ENGINEERING EVOLUTIONS

Beating Natural Disasters

From Ancient Survival to a Disaster-Proof Future

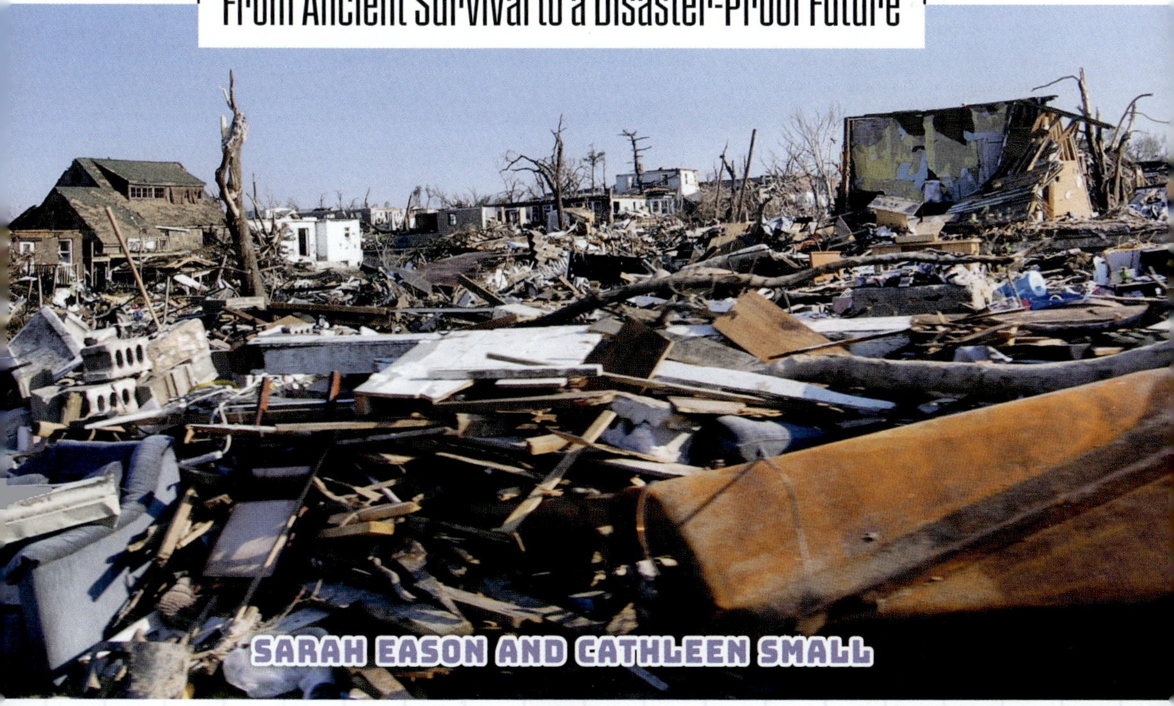

SARAH EASON AND CATHLEEN SMALL

CHERITON
CHILDREN'S BOOKS

Published in 2026 by Cheriton Children's Books
1 Bank Drive West, Shrewsbury, Shropshire, SY3 9DJ, UK

© Copyright 2026 Cheriton Children's Books

First Edition

Authors: Sarah Eason and Cathleen Small
Editor: Jennifer Sanderson
Designer: Paul Myerscough
Proofreader: Ellie Truman

Picture credits: Cover: Shutterstock/Gorodenkoff (left), Shutterstock/Andrei Armiagov (right). Inside: p1: Shutterstock/Wynn Photography, p4: Shutterstock/Triff, p5: Shutterstock/Mohammad Bash, p6: Shutterstock/Bilanol, p7: Shutterstock/Fotokita, p8: Shutterstock/Designua, p9t: Shutterstock/Designua, p9b: Shutterstock/Wirestock Creators, p10t: Shutterstock/Domenichini Giuliano, p10b: Shutterstock/Wynn Photography, p11: Shutterstock/Triff, p12: Shutterstock/Newtonian, p13: Shutterstock/Jose Carlos Alexandre, p14: Shutterstock/Marcos E Ramos Ponciano, p15t: Shutterstock, p15c: Shutterstock/Chewy Bacca, p16: Shutterstock/Lachlan von Nubia, p17: Shutterstock/AI Generator, pp18–19: Shutterstock/Timofeev Vladimir, p20: Shutterstock/AnnaNel, p21: Shutterstock/Belikova Oksana, p23t: Shutterstock/Langgong Vectorist, p23r: Shutterstock/A. L. Spangler, p23b: Shutterstock/Cowardlion, p24: Shutterstock/Damsea, p24br: Shutterstock/Petroleum Man, p25: Shutterstock/Everett Collection, pp26–27: Shutterstock/Artsiom P, p28: Shutterstock, p29: Shutterstock/Aapsky, p30: Shutterstock/George Trumpeter, p31: Shutterstock/Langkawi, p32t: Shutterstock/Ungvar, p32bl: NOAA/NMFS/OST/Allen Shimada, pp32–33: Shutterstock/Toa55, p34: Shutterstock/Sakarin Sawasdinaka, p35t: Shutterstock/Michael Vi, p35b: Shutterstock/Alaskagirl8821, p36t: Shutterstock/Aapsky, p36b_Sampling by Volcanologist, p37: Shutterstock/elRoce, p38: US Geological Survey/Washington State University/Jet Propulsion Laboratory/California Institute of Technology, p39: US Geological Survey, p40: Shutterstock/Adam Constanza, p41: Shutterstock/Adam Constanza, p42t: Shutterstock/Eric1207cvb, p42bl: Shutterstock/Holger Kleine, p42br: Shutterstock/Christopher PB, p43: Shutterstock/Rizky Novan Sinarta, p44: Shutterstock/KingShopArt, p45: Shutterstock/Jared Farrer, p46: U.S. Air Force/Tech. Sgt. James Pritchett, p47: NOAA/U.S. Air Force/Senior Airman Anna-Marie Wyant, p48: Shutterstock/Bilanol, p49: Shutterstock/Jean Faucett, p50: Shutterstock/Mohammad Bash, p51: Shutterstock/AI Generator, p52: Shutterstock/Photoongraphy, pp54–55: Shutterstock/PPR109103, p56: Shutterstock/Bell Ka Pang, p57: Shutterstock/Artur Sarkisyan, p58: Shutterstock/BigPixel Photo.

All rights reserved. No part of this book may be reproduced in any form without permission of the publisher, except by a reviewer.

Printed in China

Please visit our website,
www.cheritonchildrensbooks.com
to see more of our high-quality books.

CONTENTS

EVOLUTIONS IN ENGINEERING

Engineering is the use of scientific, mathematical, and practical ideas to design and create things such as buildings, machines, and devices to solve problems and improve people's lives. The people who come up with ideas for these buildings, machines, and devices are engineers. We have engineers to thank for the many innovations in natural disaster management that have happened throughout the ages, from building dams that help prevent flooding to early-warning systems for hurricanes and tornadoes.

Natural Disasters and Where They Happen

A natural disaster is a natural event that causes a lot of damage and can injure or kill many people. There are many types of natural disasters, from volcanoes and earthquakes to hurricanes and tornadoes. Some natural disasters are more common than others—around the world, there are fewer volcanic eruptions than hurricanes.

Some parts of the world experience more natural disasters than others. For example, the Pacific Ring of Fire is an area that has a lot of volcanoes. It also experiences a great deal of tectonic plate movement, which can result in earthquakes and tsunamis. The central United States is prone to a lot of tornadoes, so much so that it is named Tornado Alley. Other parts of the world, such as Southeast Asia, experience a lot of floods. Wildfires ravage many areas too, including parts of North America, Europe, and Australia.

Hurricanes are among the natural disasters that strike around the world.

Engineering Past, Present, and Future

Natural disasters have always caused catastrophe for humans. Earthquakes and floods have wiped out entire settlements, so too have wildfires and volcanoes. Disasters have destroyed crops and caused starvation. Throughout the ages, engineers have come up with solutions to help people manage natural disasters. These include three main areas: prediction, protection, and response. When natural disasters can be predicted, it gives people more time to prepare and move to a safer place. Although we cannot stop natural disasters, we can use engineering to help protect ourselves against them. That includes creating buildings and other structures that have defenses against natural disasters. Engineering also helps us respond to natural disasters in ways that save lives.

An earthquake that hit Syria and Turkey in 2023 caused catastrophic damage.

An Engineering Evolution

In this book, we'll explore engineering that has helped us deal with natural disasters through history, from earliest times to the present day. We'll discover how engineering has evolved and why ancient engineering has inspired modern engineering. We'll learn how engineers have come up with smart ways to solve the current issues around natural disasters. We'll also explore the exciting developments in engineering that are just around the corner as we move toward a future impacted by climate change, and the effect that may have on natural disasters.

CHAPTER 1

UNDERSTANDING DISASTERS

Natural disasters have always been part of our world. They have been such significant events that people have recorded them since early times. In fact, natural disasters have been so devastating that many ancient cultures believed they were signs that their gods were angry with them. Today, we better understand natural disasters and what causes them, thanks to advances in science.

What Is a Flood?

A flood occurs when water covers usually dry land. There are five main categories of flood: river floods, coastal floods, storm surges, inland floods, and flash floods.

- **River floods:** These can happen because of very heavy rainfall or snowmelt. They can also occur when the river's normal path becomes blocked. The amount of water becomes too much for the riverbed to handle. As a result, the water rises over the riverbanks and spills onto the surrounding land.
- **Coastal floods:** These floods occur when the sea or ocean rises above its usual level and spills over barriers, such as levees or dunes, onto dry land. The rising water can be due to tides that are higher than usual or a result of storm activity.
- **Storm surges:** These are high tides that spill over onto dry land because of three factors: wind, waves, and low atmospheric pressure. Storm surge is a big concern during hurricanes, which have all three of the above factors.
- **Inland floods:** These types of floods occur in inland areas, and they are usually caused by heavy rainfall or snowmelt.
- **Flash floods:** These floods happen very quickly and can be the result of sudden heavy rainfall or the result of a dam or levee break, for example. They are extremely dangerous because they can occur with little warning and are very powerful.

This flooding in Florida was caused by a storm surge.

Tsunamis can reach huge proportions. In the past, giant tsunamis have wiped out communities of people who lived in settlements along shorelines.

Understanding Tsunamis

A tsunami is a series of towering, powerful ocean waves. Tsunamis can be caused by earthquakes on the ocean floor. The ocean earthquakes can cause huge amounts of water above them to become displaced, or moved, which can result in tsunamis. The giant waves can also be created when large bodies of ice or rock fall into an area of water, such as a lake, sea, or ocean. That too displaces water and creates huge waves that can cause devastation.

Tsunamis are not like ordinary waves. Ordinary waves can reach huge heights, but they break and curl over as they reach the shore. Tsunamis do not stop or slow down as they travel, and they do not break at coasts. Instead, they hit land as tall, solid walls of water. They also continue to move at speed. A tsunami is an unstoppable force. It sweeps away anything in its path and can change a coastline in a matter of minutes.

What Is a Wildfire?

A wildfire is when a natural area of land—often a forest, grassland, or prairie—catches fire. The flames then quickly spread and get out of control. They can travel across a wide area. Large wildfires can cause terrible damage to plants, animals, people, and property. Some wildfires can be huge and burn more than 100,000 acres (40,470 ha) of land. The flames of such a fire can measure 150 feet (46 m) high.

Understanding Earthquakes

Earth's surface is covered in a crust that is made up of tectonic plates. These plates are like pieces of a jigsaw puzzle. They all come together to form the top layer of Earth. Between these plates are seams, just like there are seams where puzzle pieces come together. These seams are called plate boundaries, and they are points at which the plates move. There are three main types of plate boundaries, and the plates there move in different ways:

- **Transform boundaries:** At these points plates move and slide past each other. This causes cracks in Earth's crust. These cracks are known as faults.

- **Divergent boundaries:** These are points at which tectonic plates move away from each other. This can cause faults in the crust too. Beneath the ocean, those faults are called mid-ocean ridges. On dry land, they are called rift valleys.

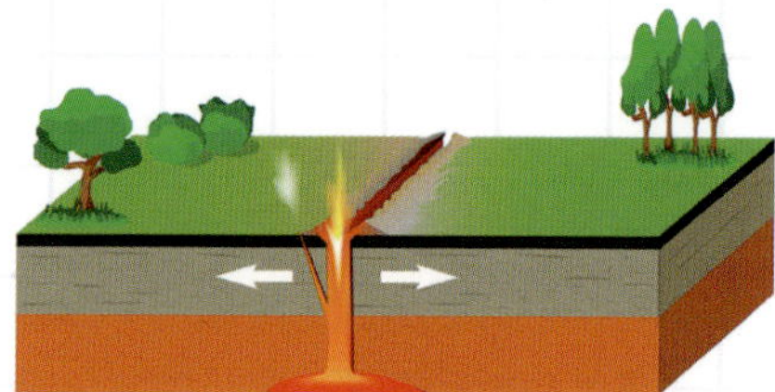

- **Convergent boundaries:** In these areas, plates move toward each other. The plates push against or slide over each other.

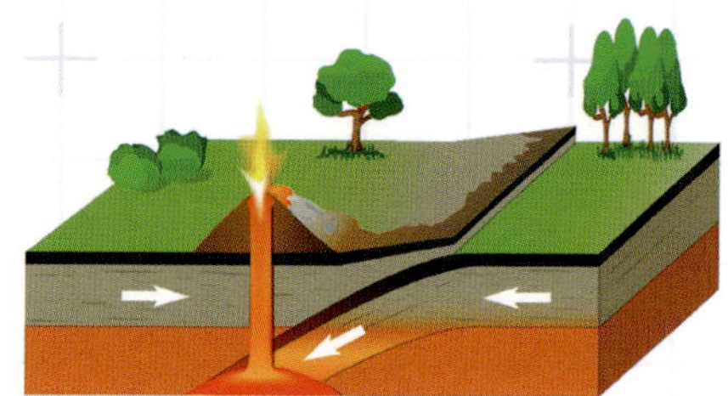

What Is a Volcano?

Volcanoes are vents, or openings, in Earth's surface. Beneath these vents are enormous amounts of molten, or melted, rock called magma. Volcanoes can remain peaceful for hundreds and even thousands of years. However, if magma builds up beneath Earth's surface, the pressure of the buildup can sometimes become too great. Then, the magma either explodes or seeps out onto the surface. This is an eruption.

HOW IT WORKS:
AN EARTHQUAKE

As the tectonic plates move, some slipping and bumping can occur. That slipping and bumping causes minor trembling in the earth, which helps release tension between the plates. However, the plates can sometimes become stuck. When that happens, the tension builds up in the form of energy. The plates continue to try to move, and eventually they become unstuck. The tension that built up when the plates became lodged is then released and causes an earthquake.

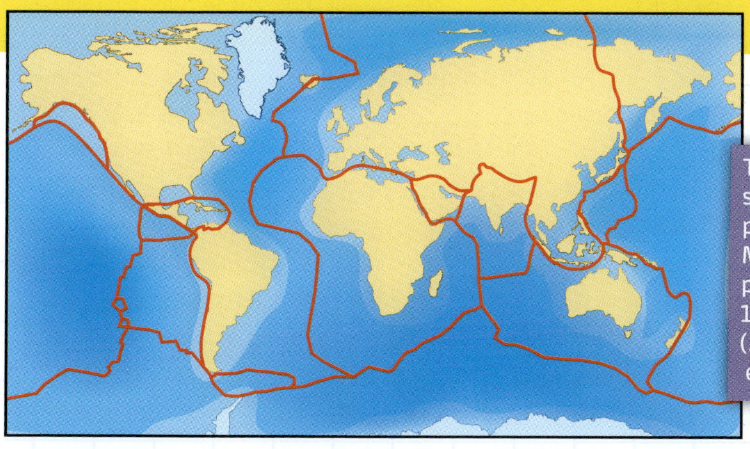

This diagram shows Earth's plate boundaries. Most tectonic plates move 1 to 2 inches (2.5 to 5 cm) each year.

Mauna Loa in Hawaii is one of Earth's most active volcanoes.

Tornadoes are characterized by a long funnel of swirling air that extends from the cloud to the ground.

Studying Tornadoes

Tornadoes are columns of air that reach from a thunderstorm to the ground and rotate, or spin, violently. Air is invisible, so this means that sometimes tornadoes cannot be seen right away. However, as soon as they pick up water droplets from the storm and dust and debris from the ground, they become visible as swirling columns. These columns move quickly across the landscape.

Scientists have collected data that explains how tornadoes often form. First, a specific type of thunderstorm called a supercell develops. Supercells are different from regular thunderstorms because within them, they have a rotating updraft. This swirling mass of air is called the mesocyclone. Supercell storms do not always spawn tornadoes. Scientists think that most tornadoes form based on temperature differences between the downdraft air and the mesocyclone. However, data they have collected suggests that sometimes tornadoes form even when there are no significant differences in temperature.

Joplin, Missouri, was devastated by a massive 2011 tornado.

Understanding Tropical Cyclones

Tropical cyclones are storms that form over tropical and subtropical water. When sustained winds are less than 39 miles per hour (63 kph), the storm is called a tropical depression. When winds are more than 39 miles per hour (63 kph), the weather event becomes a tropical storm. And when winds are greater than 74 miles per hour (119 kph), the storm is a hurricane.

Inside the Eye

At the center of the hurricane, the air sinks and forms a roughly circular area known as the "eye." The storm systems rotate around the eye of the storm. The eye is mostly cloud-free and does not have strong winds or rain. It is relatively calm compared to the bands around the eye. There the winds are intense and thunderstorms occur.

Seen from satellite imagery, a hurricane looks like a giant swirling mass of clouds.

HOW IT WORKS: A HURRICANE

Hurricanes are fed by the warm tropical waters where they form. Water of 79 degrees Fahrenheit (26 °C) or higher tends to fuel hurricanes. As the thunderstorms that start hurricanes move over the warm tropical or subtropical waters, they suck up moisture and water vapor. That rising water vapor creates more clouds and more thunderstorms. That continuing cycle of cloud and thunderstorm creation causes the hurricane to grow in size and power. The water vapor condenses into water droplets, which releases some of the warmth and further adds to the storm, increasing its power.

A category 5 tornado caused this destruction in Moore, Oklahoma, in 2013.

Measuring Disaster

Engineers have come up with some ingenious ways to help us measure the scale and force of natural disasters. These systems enable us to figure out how big some natural disasters, such as tornadoes and hurricanes, are likely to be before they strike. Others help us measure the impact of the disaster, such as an earthquake, after it has hit.

Tornado and Hurricane Ratings

Tornadoes are rated based on the Enhanced Fujita Scale (EF-Scale), which the National Weather Service began to use in 2007. The EF-Scale works backward to estimate a tornado's strength. It looks at the damage caused by the tornado and uses the data from 28 damage indicators and 8 degrees of damage. From that information it figures out the tornado's wind speed. The EF-Scale rates tornadoes from 0 to 5 based on the windspeed of the storm. A tornado that is 0 on the EF-Scale has wind gusts measured at 65 to 85 miles per hour (104 to 136 kph). A tornado that is 5 on the EF-Scale has wind gusts measured at 200 to 234 miles per hour (321 to 376 kph).

Hurricane wind speeds for a Category 5 hurricane are greater than 157 miles per hour (252 kph). Hurricane measurements look at sustained windspeeds, whereas tornado measurements look at wind gusts. So a tornado has stronger winds than a hurricane, but in gusts. Whereas a hurricane's winds are more sustained.

Measuring Earthquakes

The place directly above where an earthquake starts is called the epicenter. That is where the worst of the shaking is felt. Most damage takes place here, but the energy released by an earthquake spreads out in every direction. It spreads through the ground and causes ripples, like those seen on a pond when a stone is thrown into it. The energy travels in the form of shock waves, which are called seismic waves. First, they shake the crust. When they reach Earth's surface, they shake everything on the ground. Engineers have created a useful tool to help us monitor and measure seismic waves: the seismometer.

Seismic waves can cause powerful, intense shuddering of the ground. The movements can be so violent that they cause buildings to crumble.

HOW IT WORKS:

A SEISMOMETER

A seismometer is a little like a pendulum on a fixed base. A weight at the end of the pendulum swings as the ground shakes. The more it shakes, the faster the pendulum swings. A network of seismometers exists around the world. They record seismic waves in their locations. By recording the times at which seismic waves pass each location, scientists can figure out the epicenter of an earthquake.

Measuring the Energy of Earthquakes

Scientists also measure how much energy an earthquake releases. The measure of energy is called magnitude. Most scientists today use a system called Moment Magnitude Scale (MMS). It measures the size of the shock waves during an earthquake. Each step in the scale is 10 times greater than the previous number. The most powerful earthquake ever recorded was a magnitude of 9.5. It took place in Chile, South America, in 1960.

CHAPTER 2

A HISTORY OF NATURAL DISASTERS

There is a lot of evidence of smart engineering in early human history to help manage natural disasters. Countless powerful natural events have harmed humans since earliest time. But ancient people came up with resourceful ways to protect themselves from these natural disasters.

Holding Back the Water and Going Higher

The ancient Egyptians and Mesopotamians built dikes and levees made of earth. They positioned them along riverbanks to hold back rising water. The structures directed floodwater away from settlements, thereby protecting their buildings and inhabitants. Ancient people also built their settlements on higher ground in areas that were frequently flooded. For example, the Indus Valley Civilization built cities on raised mounds to protect them from nearby rivers. The ancient Chinese cut canals to divert water from the Yellow River, to prevent it flooding their settlements. And they also built homes on platforms to protect them from the frequent flooding of the river.

The Nile River regularly bursts its banks and floods surrounding land.

Working with Nature

People who lived along coastal areas of Japan and China in early times worked with natural barriers to help provide defense against surging ocean water, such as storm surges and tsunamis. Rather than cutting down forests around coastal areas, they protected them and kept them in place. In return, the trees acted as a line of defense when a natural disaster such as a storm surge hit. The people along coastal areas created raised mounds and built houses in elevated positions to protect against flooding. They also kept evacuation boats nearby, so they could quickly escape if waters became too high.

The Tigris River is a large and powerful waterway.

The Yellow River snakes across China's landscape.

BIG Breakthroughs

Smart early civilizations even found a way to benefit from floodwater—by building reservoirs to hold the excess water. The ancient Egyptians built banks of earth to create large basins that would hold water, much like reservoirs do today. They dug channels from the Nile River to direct floodwater into these basins. By doing so, they were able to capture the seasonal floodwaters of the Nile River and then later use it during drier periods.

People in Mesopotamia had similar systems. They built canals from the Tigris and Euphrates Rivers to direct the water toward their fields of crops. That ensured their crops were regularly watered while also reducing the risk of the rivers flooding their nearby settlements.

A Fear of Fire

Living alongside the awesome forces of nature that are wildfires demanded some smart thinking and engineering strategy. Historically, people worked with nature to outsmart fires. And many of the engineering techniques they thought up are still used today. Indigenous people living in North America and Australia often used controlled burns to protect themselves and their settlements from wildfires. They intentionally created small fires in places that might easily catch fire during a wildfire. They then controlled the burn, allowing it to clear crisp, dry vegetation that could catch alight during a natural fire. The same techniques are used today in areas that are at risk of wildfire.

This building in Egypt is made of mudbricks. The practice of building with these ancient forms of bricks is still used today in some parts of the world, including Africa and Asia.

BIG Breakthroughs

Figuring out what materials were easily flammable, and which were not, was a game-changer for fighting fire. People in ancient times quickly became aware of building materials that could easily catch alight. In places where wildfires were a threat, they took care to build with fire-resistant materials, such as mudbrick.

Mudbrick and stone were commonly used in ancient construction because they resist fire and extreme temperatures. Mudbricks, made from clay, silt, and straw, absorb and store heat without catching fire. This is because they have high thermal mass, meaning they take in heat slowly and release it gradually. Stone, like limestone and granite, is also naturally fire-resistant and does not burn. These materials helped ancient civilizations build structures that could withstand heat and wildfires.

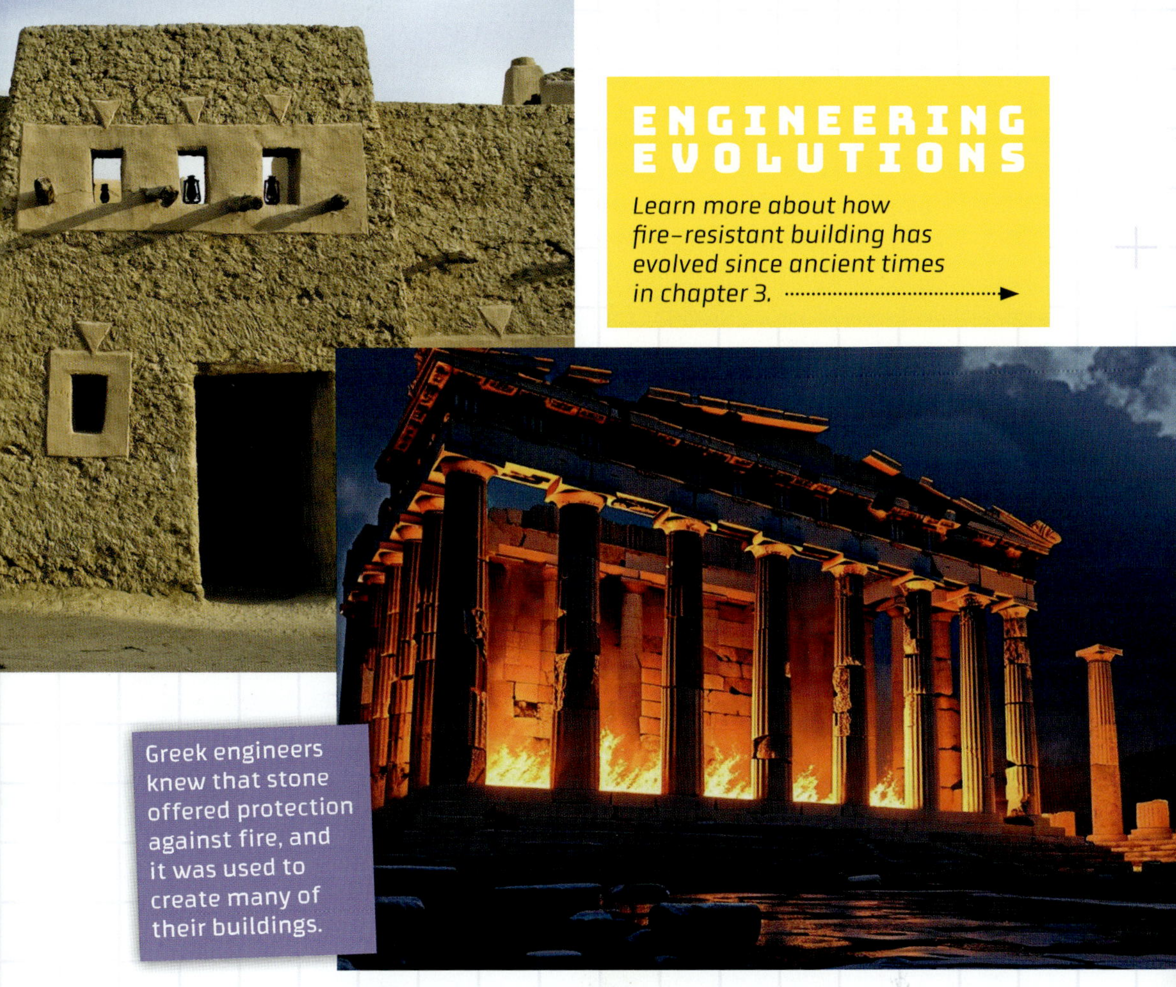

ENGINEERING EVOLUTIONS

Learn more about how fire-resistant building has evolved since ancient times in chapter 3.

Greek engineers knew that stone offered protection against fire, and it was used to create many of their buildings.

Using Nature for Protection

A firebreak is a gap in vegetation or other material that can easily burn. The gap acts as a barrier to slow or stop the fire. People used natural firebreaks for protection against wildfires. They settled near streams, lakes, rivers, and rocky outcrops that could provide natural firebreaks during a wildfire. Animals such as goats and sheep were often used to keep down grasses and shrubs, which could easily catch fire. These domestic animals were allowed to graze land around settlements, eating away at vegetation that could otherwise provide food for fires.

Rules and Warnings

The Romans even put laws, or codes, in place for building with materials that were not flammable. The building codes included using materials such as stone and clay because they do not easily catch fire. They also included good ventilation systems to help protect people from smoke inhalation in the event of a fire.

The smart engineers of ancient Greece and Rome also set up fire lookouts, to watch out for fires. Tall towers were built that allowed the person inside to watch for fire. The watchers could quickly spot a fire, and alert communities.

Deadly Volcanoes and Epic Earthquakes

Volcanic eruptions and earthquakes are some of the deadliest and most violent of natural disasters. Like humans today, early people had few defenses against these forces of nature. However, they did have useful strategies that helped them predict the disasters and try to protect against them—and they even came up with ways to benefit from them.

Some of the buildings of the city of Knossos are still standing, which shows how well engineered they were to withstand Earth's powerful movements.

First Early Warning and Protection

Ancient people learned to recognize the signs of volcanic eruptions. They noted changes in animal behavior, such as flocks of birds rapidly leaving an area. They paid attention to ground tremors, which could indicate an eruption was on the way. They noticed the smell of sulfur, a gas given off by volcanoes. If they spotted these signs, they would move communities to safer places.

BIG Breakthroughs

There is evidence that after volcanic eruptions or earthquakes had taken place, the ancient Greeks and Romans rebuilt towns with clear escape routes for people to take if another disaster took place. This smart civic planning gave people a faster, safer means of escape and would have saved lives. Towns and cities were also designed with large, open central spaces called plazas. Although the plazas were designed for the purpose of giving people a place to meet, they also provided "safe zones" during a disaster. In plazas, people would be less likely to be trapped beneath falling buildings and rubble.

Benefiting from Disaster

Inventive humans discovered that while volcanic eruptions could be deadly, they could also be life-giving. In many volcanic places, after an eruption, a rich, fertile soil is created. That is because lava contains many minerals that are nutritious for crops. Ancient farmers discovered that by planting crops on the hillsides near volcanoes, they could benefit from the nutrient-rich soil there. This practice still takes place today in many volcanic places, including on the hillsides near Mount Vesuvius in Italy.

Engineering for Earthquakes

The ancient Greeks and Romans not only created escape routes in their towns and cities, but they also thought ahead about how they could make their buildings better able to withstand earthquakes. Buildings were reinforced to make them less likely to collapse. The ancient Greeks and Romans also began to use gravel as a foundation, and the Romans also used cement. Gravel slightly shifts during an earthquake, and easily absorbs shock. By using it for foundations, the likelihood of buildings collapsing was reduced.

There is evidence that the Minoan civilization developed better methods of building after disastrous earthquakes hit their cities. The ruins of the Minoan city of Knossos show that flexible wooden beams were built into walls. The beams helped absorb some of the shocks of earthquakes and stopped the walls collapsing. The Minoans also built with large, irregular stones. That provided extra stability and strength, which helped keep buildings standing during earthquakes.

ENGINEERING EVOLUTIONS

Discover how management after natural disasters has developed in chapter 6. →

Pyramid Protection

The pyramids of the ancient Egyptians, Maya, and Aztecs are famous for their awe-inspiring architecture. These impressive designs were built for religious purposes, but also had an additional benefit: They were able to withstand earthquakes. Structures with wider bases and walls that taper as they go upward are more stable. They are less likely to collapse when the ground moves. Ancient people may have been aware of this when they created pyramid-shaped structures. Many are still standing today, which is proof of their strength and durability.

Built to Sway

In earthquake-prone places such as Japan, people traditionally built structures with wooden frameworks. Wood can more easily bend and absorb shock more effectively than rigid materials such as stone. The wooden structures coped better if an earthquake hit and were less likely to collapse. Bamboo was often used for building. That is because it is incredibly lightweight and flexible. Structures made from bamboo tend to sway rather than collapse during an earthquake.

Super Shock Absorbers

Peru is prone to earthquakes. The Incas who lived there from the thirteenth century to the sixteenth century came up with smart ways of building with stone to protect their settlements from earthquakes. The system is called ashlar masonry. The Incas built with interlocking stone blocks but did not use mortar. Mortar acts as a kind of glue between blocks, holding them together. However, it can easily crumble during an earthquake. By removing the mortar but fitting the blocks tightly, they absorbed shock well during earthquakes. That made the buildings of settlements such as Machu Picchu amazingly tough. The remains of the structures are still standing today.

ENGINEERING EVOLUTIONS

Find out how engineering to manage earthquakes has evolved in chapter 4. →

These are the famous pyramids at Giza, Egypt. The structures are thousands of years old.

The extraordinary engineering achievements of the Inca mean that parts of Machu Picchu can still be seen today.

HOW IT WORKS: ASHLAR MASONRY

Ashlar masonry is constructed using this process:

Shaping the stone: Each stone block was carefully shaped to fit tightly with the other stones that surrounded it.

Spreading the weight: The stones were wider at the bottom and narrower at the top. That meant weight was more evenly distributed, and the stones were less likely to topple during an earthquake.

Moving puzzle pieces: When an earthquake hit, the stones could flex slightly because they were not joined by mortar. They moved a little like puzzle pieces, coming apart slightly then joining together again. When the earthquake passed, they settled back into place once more.

A Slow-Down in Discovery

In the centuries that followed ancient times, there were some pretty limited developments in engineering to protect against natural disasters. Ancient peoples such as the Egyptians, Greeks, Romans, and Maya were very inventive and advanced for their time. Many of the engineering methods they had employed continued to be used until Medieval times. Systems of building levees and drainage systems continued. In some earthquake-prone places, buildings were reinforced. And in some coastal areas of Europe, such as Britain, thick walls were created to help protect against the often-frequent sea storms that ravaged coastal areas.

An Explosion of Ideas

It wasn't really until the Renaissance, which began in the fifteenth century, and the Age of Enlightenment, which began in the seventeenth century, that people began to come up with new engineering to help guard against natural disasters. During these eras, the world of science exploded with ideas, and communication of those thoughts spread rapidly. People began to study natural disasters such as earthquakes and volcanoes. Engineers began to focus on reinforcing buildings against disasters such as earthquakes. They returned to using heavy, stable foundations and reinforced frames inspired by building techniques of the ancient Greeks and Romans.

Engineers in what is now the Netherlands, Europe, created advanced levee systems. They also came up with water pumps and windmill-driven drainage systems. These helped people not only protect against floods but also reclaim land from the sea. They then used that land to farm and build on. Large reservoirs and dams were also built to prevent flooding into settlements downstream.

ENGINEERING EVOLUTIONS

Learn more about how flood engineering has evolved in chapter 3. ►

Earthquake-Proof Building

When a major earthquake took place in Lisbon, Portugal, in 1755, it changed building there forever. A tsunami also hit the coast, with up to 66-feet-high (20 m) waves. It killed thousands of people. The overall death toll because of the disasters is estimated at between 10,000 and 50,000 people. The quake was so disastrous that it prompted a greater awareness of natural disasters and a need to protect against them.

After the earthquake event in Portugal, the country's prime minister led the rebuilding of Lisbon. He did so with designs that would make buildings less likely to collapse during an earthquake. That included flexible wooden-framed structures and frameworks that absorbed seismic shock. The city was also reconstructed with wider streets. That meant if buildings did topple, they were less likely to take down surrounding structures too.

Meanwhile, on the other side of the world in Asia, other developments were underway. Between the seventeenth and nineteenth centuries, Japanese engineers were using ingenious joinery to create buildings. It was called mortise and tenon joinery and was designed to be incredibly flexible and could sway easily during an earthquake.

HOW IT WORKS:

MORTISE AND TENON JOINERY

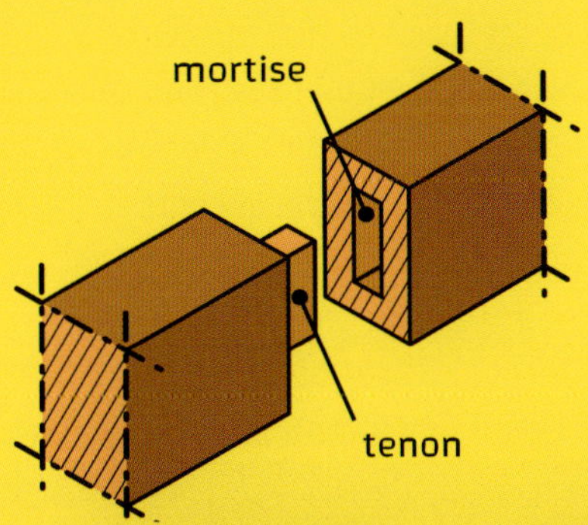

This traditional joinery system is so effective that it is still used in Japan today. This is how it works:

Snug and flexible connections: A pointed part of one piece of timber, called a tenon, fits into a hole in another part of a piece of timber, called a mortise.

Moving without breaking: The two pieces fit snugly together yet during any seismic activity, they can slightly move without breaking. Unlike nails or other metal fasteners, they do not snap. They also allow the rest of the wood to easily move then return into position, fitting snugly again.

Mortise and tenon joinery fixes pieces of wood together in a way that allows a degree of movement.

The Japanese also created wooden buildings called pagodas using mortise and tenon joinery. The buildings bend and flex with earth tremors. Even at five stories high, they can withstand earthquakes.

Protection from Storms

Building to protect against storms has a long and ancient history. Coastal communities, such as those in the Caribbean and the Gulf Coast, built homes on stilts to try and protect them from storm surges. And people in Central America and Southeast Asia often used local materials such as thatch, bamboo, or palm materials to create roofs that were flexible and less likely to break during a hurricane. Buildings that were low to the ground were used, with steep, sloping roofs that the wind could easily bounce off. Most had small openings, such as little windows and doors, which could also more easily withstand damage from wind.

The practice of building low-to-the-ground thatched huts is still used today in hurricane-prone parts of the world, such as Central America.

BIG Breakthroughs

A barometer

In the seventeenth and eighteenth centuries, people began to study weather with greater scientific understanding. During this time, they invented devices such as the barometer and thermometer. These tools paved the way for measuring and predicting storms and wind pressure. These were the first steps toward accurate weather forecasting. They were also steps toward predicting storms such as hurricanes and tornadoes. Early scientists also began to monitor earth tremors, gas emissions, and changes in temperature around volcanoes. That allowed them to make predictions about eruptions, and evacuate people ahead of them.

Shutting Out the Storm

Building to protect against storms continued into the nineteenth century, when European settlers in hurricane-prone places started to use storm shutters for windows. They could be tightly shut during storms to prevent windows breaking. In tornado-prone places in the American Midwest, people began building storm cellars, dugouts, and other underground shelters to protect them from the terrifying storms. These were safe places in which to wait out the fast-moving disasters that ripped up structures at ground level.

New Ways to Deal with Disaster

By the early twentieth century, engineers were finding new, inventive ways to protect people from natural disasters. Buildings made of steel-reinforced concrete allowed high-rise structures that could withstand storm damage and earthquakes. This was particularly important after devastating earthquakes destroyed great parts of cities, including the San Francisco disaster of 1906.

As the twentieth century unfolded, new and improved engineering methods to deal with disaster unfolded too. They included bigger and stronger dams, including the Hoover Dam. New flood projects, such as the Mississippi River Levee system were developed. Improved underground shelters and safe rooms were created to help people survive tornadoes.

Advances in meteorology, or weather study and forecasting, also meant that people were better able to track storms and warn people before they struck.

Twenty-First Century Solutions

As we make our way through the twenty-first century, climate change and the impact it is having on natural disasters is a real concern. Global warming is bringing about more natural disasters than we faced in the past. However, while global climate change is making natural disasters increasingly common, engineers are helping us learn to live alongside these awesome forces of nature.

Rebuilding practices after epic earthquakes such as the one that hit San Francisco in 1906 tried to future-proof against disasters.

ENGINEERING EVOLUTIONS

Learn more about engineering for weather prediction in chapter 5. →

CHAPTER 3

FLOODS, TSUNAMIS, AND WILDFIRES

Floods, tsunamis, and wildfires cause devastation, but modern engineering is helping us better predict when some of these natural disasters are likely to hit, and where. With forewarning, people can be evacuated from danger zones, and lives saved. We are also becoming better at building structures that can handle natural disasters, and better at putting systems in place to provide the help that people need afterward in order to recover from disaster.

Studies from Space

One of the engineering game-changers that has transformed how we monitor floods, tsunamis, and wildfires are satellites. These are objects that are sent into orbit to circle our planet. They send images and information back to computers on Earth. Some satellites keep track of the weather on Earth by watching it from above. These satellites have cameras that take images of Earth's atmosphere. They show where thick clouds that might bring rain are forming, which could result in flooding. They also show where thunderstorms could occur, bringing lightning that could spark a fire. The satellites also highlight high temperatures, low humidity, and high winds, all of which are linked to wildfires.

Fixed and Moving

Weather satellites in geostationary orbits stay in one place high above Earth's surface. They sit 22,400 miles (36,050 km) above the equator. Other satellites circle over the North Pole to the South Pole and back again. They travel as close to the surface as 435 miles (700 km). They take detailed pictures of weather patterns all over the world. Those images help us track changes in weather that could result in floods or wildfires.

Satellites help us track weather activity on Earth.

ENGINEERING SOLUTIONS

There is no sunlight at night, which makes nighttime monitoring of weather by satellite image difficult. To overcome that problem, engineers have created satellites with special sensors that can measure heat. Infrared images show where clouds are because they are always colder than the land and water below. Clouds with very cold tops bring the greatest risk because they can bring heavy rainfall and are a threat for flooding. The heat-measuring sensors on the satellites mean that weather—and potential natural disasters—can be monitored throughout day and night.

Tsunami Tracking

Radar satellites are particularly important when it comes to tracking tsunamis. These satellites can help measure the height of a tsunami wave. Equipment on each satellite creates measurements by sending pulses from space to the surface of Earth's oceans. The speed of the pulses, the position of the satellite, and the time the pulses take to return to the satellite are measured and analyzed. Scientists can then use the data to figure out the height of the ocean's surface and note areas where it is particularly high. That can indicate a tsunami is forming and heading to shore.

Looking from the Sky

Satellite images are particularly useful for monitoring how much water there is in the upper layers of Earth's atmosphere. Water vapor images show where heavy rain that could lead to flooding is possible. The more water vapor there is in the air, the heavier the rain that is likely to follow. Water vapor satellite pictures show wetter areas as white, with drier places dark.

Ocean buoys work by transmitting data from sensors on the seabed to warning centers positioned on land.

HOW IT WORKS: AN OCEAN SENSOR

Sensors are important for monitoring water flow in rivers and streams, and they are also used for monitoring the water of the oceans. Figuring out what is happening far out in the world's enormous oceans is tricky. But using sensors has made it a lot easier. Sensors on the ocean floor help us watch out for tsunamis. The sensors record any change in water pressure when a tsunami passes over them. That data is sent to a buoy on the ocean surface. The buoy uses a satellite to send the information to a warning center, which then alerts people to the danger.

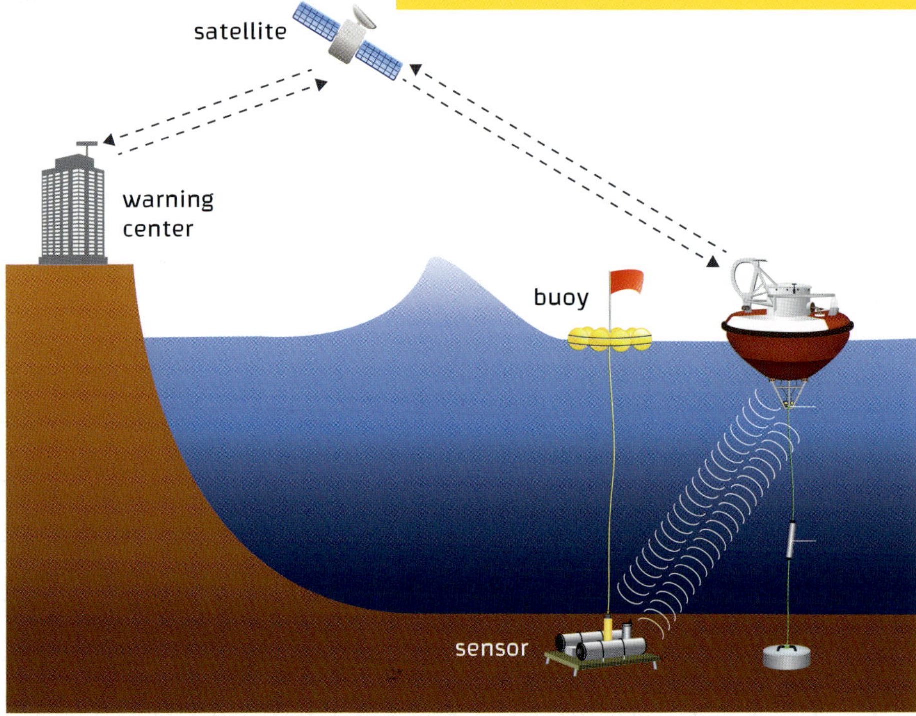

Looking from Land

Checking flood risk from land is also important. Engineering tools such as rain gauges and sensors in streams and rivers makes flood monitoring far more accurate today. The Iowa Flood Center (IFC) is devoted to flood research in the United States. It oversees a network of stream and river sensors. The IFC collects data about water levels. It also maintains weather stations and rain gauges across the state. The gauges collect rainfall. The weather stations gather data on wind direction and speed. They also measure moisture in the soil, the level of ground water, and temperature. All that data is then used to create real-time flood forecasts.

Mapping and Modeling

LiDAR stands for light detection and ranging. It works by using the light from pulsed lasers to measure distances and elevation, or height. Some cities are using LiDAR to create accurate elevation maps for the city. That helps engineers know where to focus their efforts for flood prevention. Another way engineers help communities prepare for flooding is by using computer modeling. Data about areas that are at risk of flooding is fed into a computer. Programs then use that data to simulate, or show, what would happen if the area received heavy rainfall. Engineers can use these simulations to make decisions about where to position flood defenses, such as stormwater drainage and retention ponds.

Using a New Intelligence

Artificial intelligence (AI) is revolutionizing how people deal with floods. AI learns from past information and then puts what it has learned into action. Autodesk's Machine Learning Deluge tool uses AI learned from the data of 10,000 flood simulations. That knowledge is applied to create simulations of how different terrain could be affected by a flood—all in the fraction of the time it would take a human to do the same job.

Improved satellite monitoring of the surface of Earth's oceans could help us spot tsunamis.

Back to Basics

Just as our tools for monitoring and predicting flooding have improved, so too have our means of managing floods. As people in ancient times used levees, channels, floodwalls, dams, and reservoirs to protect against floodwater, so too do engineers today. But in improved ways.

Building Better

With increasing risk of flooding, engineers are widening and deepening many river channels to deal with the extra water. Levees are built bigger and from stronger materials, such as concrete, which are more likely to withstand the pounding of water. Engineers are also building both permanent and temporary water storage basins to manage stormwater runoff. The basins collect additional water on the ground caused by heavy rainfall. That lessens the amount that then runs into rivers and streams, which reduces the risk of flooding.

Drones on the Lookout

Another smart solution engineers have developed to manage drainage is using drones to scan for obstacles in drainage systems. Drones can go into sewers and stormwater drains to look for blockages, and do so much faster than people.

Green Engineering

Engineers are also working with nature rather than against it. Green engineering focuses on sustainable ways to manage flooding. One green way to manage stormwater is to create pavements that absorb water, rather than have it simply run off the surface. Pavements created from porous material absorb stormwater. The stormwater drains into a stone bed or soil below the pavement. A drainage pipe in the stone bed can redirect the water to an area where it can be used for other things, such as watering gardens.

Basins like these collect and hold onto additional water that occurs during heavy rainfall.

HOW IT WORKS: A SWALE

Swales are another form of green engineering. They are wide-but-shallow channels that collect stormwater and transfer it to another area. Swales often contain stones. The water that collects in the swale seeps through the stones and into the soil below them. That provides water for the vegetation that surrounds the channel. That helps plants grow.

Swales provide eco-friendly forms of drainage.

Protecting Property

A time-old way of defending a property against flooding is using sandbags. Modern engineers have built on that traditional means of defense but made it better. They have created water-inflated property protectors that act like sandbags but are filled with water instead of sand. The protectors are stored at a person's home or business and can be quickly filled with water to create a barrier. Engineers have also designed entry barriers that act like dams to seal off doorways or other entry points, thereby protecting buildings.

Another smart invention to help protect buildings against flooding is a rapid response floodgate called Water-Gate. It is a compact device that individuals can easily set up. It uses floodwater to create a dam. When the water hits the Water-Gate, it enters cells in the barrier that push up a "wall" as the flood waters grow stronger. The weight of the water in the cells stabilizes the barrier so that it is not carried away by the floodwaters.

When the Earth Shakes

Some of the engineering systems used to watch out for earthquakes are also used to check for tsunamis. The seismometers that monitor shock waves during an earthquake can be used to monitor the shaking of the ground on the ocean floor. Powerful movements there can indicate that a tsunami could be on the way.

Drones can be used to carry out surveillance. They search for signs of fire, such as smoke, across wide areas of land.

Underwater Robots

Another engineering invention that has helped us better monitor tsunamis are autonomous underwater vehicles (AUVs). These remote-controlled robots move on their own. They follow routes programmed into their computers.

Onboard sensors record the shape and surface of the ocean floor. That information is then sent to scientists on land. It helps them figure out where tsunamis have been and what the risk of future tsunamis in those areas is likely to be.

AUVs allow us to study the seabed and locate signs of possible damage that has been caused by tsunamis.

Fleets of drones can help track the spread of a wildfire in real-time.

Wildfire Watch

Just as tracking tsunamis and warning people in good time helps save lives, so too does monitoring wildfires and alerting people in time for them to escape. The best way to watch for wildfires is from above. Engineers have come up with several smart inventions that allow us to track wildfires from the sky with greater accuracy than ever before.

Once a wildfire gains momentum, it can very easily get out of control. Key to controlling wildfires is finding them in their early stages. Satellites and sensors have made it much easier for scientists to quickly spot these dangerous natural fires. Different satellites and sensors scan various parts of wildfires. They work like cameras, taking detailed pictures of what they see. They can also make images of things humans cannot see with the naked eye. For example, they can identify and image areas that are very dry and likely to catch fire. They can show flames or the beginnings of fires, and areas of land that are already burned. They can even find moisture and other changes in the air that are caused by smoke. That information allows people to quickly see changes that indicate a wildfire, and act.

BIG Breakthroughs

Figuring out where wildfires will take place, how powerful they will be, and how quickly they will spread is key to warning people what action they should take. Engineers have created tools that help predict how quickly a wildfire will spread, and where it will spread to. Fire Area Simulator (FARSITE) is a computer model that can predict the speed and intensity of a wildfire, as well as the areas it will most affect. The model is fed with data about the landscape and weather near a fire. That helps the model figure out how much fuel the fire will have in the form of vegetation. It also helps determine how a fire will be affected by weather such as winds and dry conditions.

Walls for Waves

Some tsunami-prone countries such as Japan have developed strong sea defenses to try to protect them from the giant waves. Offshore breakwaters are structures that absorb and reduce the energy of an oncoming tsunami. They are placed out at sea, to break the force of a wave and minimize the damage it causes when it hits land. Closer to shore, tall walls made of reinforced concrete can absorb some of the power of an oncoming wave.

Riding It Out

Engineers are now exploring buildings on stilts or elevated foundations in places where tsunamis are common. The wave may pass beneath the building, reducing the risk of damage and injury to people inside. Reinforced materials such as steel and concrete are often used in areas prone to tsunamis. Both can withstand high water pressure. Lower floors of buildings that are open-plan or have breakaway walls are also helpful when dealing with tsunamis. They allow water to flow through the building, rather than hitting into a sturdy wall. That relieves the pressure on the building's foundation. As a result, the building is more likely to remain standing if a tsunami does hit.

Planning Ahead

Civic planning is also important in helping to protect against wildfires. Neighborhoods are designed with wide roads that provide easy access for emergency vehicles. They are also planned so that buildings are spread out, creating a defensible space. Areas around buildings are cleared of vegetation and designed with fire-resistant landscaping. That means using materials that are not highly flammable in structures such as fences and outdoor buildings. This smart planning helps prevent fire reaching homes and other buildings and easily passing from one building to the next.

In areas that are prone to wildfire, the materials that people use to build with are key. Using fire-resistant materials such as concrete, metal roofing, and tempered glass help reduce the risk of buildings catching fire.

Tall concrete walls in places like Japan provide some defense against powerful tsunami waves.

Not Fueling the Fire

Engineers recommend underground power lines in places where wildfires are a problem. That reduces the risk of fires being started if a line collapses or a spark flies off it. They also build in automatic shutoff systems, which cut the power when an area experiences very high winds or dry conditions. That further reduces the risk of an electrical fire leading to a wildfire. Fire hydrants, underground water tanks, and reservoirs are often installed in wildfire zones. Automatic irrigation or sprinkler systems are also put in place in wildfire hotspots. They automatically give off water to dampen down vegetation during high-risk periods.

ENGINEERING SOLUTIONS

Giving people enough time to evacuate and providing evacuation routes is vitally important if there is a threat of a wildfire or tsunami. Both move with speed, and often time to escape one is limited. Engineers have created highly sensitive early-warning systems. They provide real-time alerts to people by text, app, or siren.

A wildfire can turn from a spark to an unstoppable force, racing across dry landscapes at speeds of up to 14 miles per hour (22.5 kph)—faster than many people can run.

CHAPTER 4

VOLCANOES AND EARTHQUAKES

Studying images of volcanoes taken from above can help us spot if they are changing shape. That can be an indication of volcanic activity.

Volcanoes and earthquakes are difficult to predict. Volcanoes often show some signs of activity before an eruption, such as increased amounts of sulfur escaping from the volcano. Changes in the volcano's shape can also indicate an eruption is on the way. However, earthquakes often occur with very little warning. There are sometimes certain warning signs, such as a lot of small earthquakes in a particular area. Scientists take note of them, because it is more likely that a major earthquake will take place after a series of smaller quakes. However, there is currently no accurate early-detection system for identifying earthquakes.

Scientists who study volcanoes are called volcanologists. They visit volcanoes to find out more about how they behave. That data can help with future predictions.

BIG Breakthroughs

One technology that is showing some promise in detecting earthquakes is the use of fiber optics. Fiber optics are glass or plastic fibers that transmit, or send, information as light pulses. As the light travels along the fiber, it can detect signs such as changes in temperature. Fiber optics can capture subtle vibrations in the ground, which could indicate an earthquake is on the way.

Watching Earth

The global positioning system (GPS) is a system of satellites in space that help us figure out the position of objects on Earth. The technology can also be used to measure ground movements over time. By measuring shifts in Earth's crust, scientists can identify areas that may be at risk of earthquakes. Likewise, GPS can be used to track changes in the shape of the ground around a volcano. As magma builds up beneath the surface, the ground above may swell or tilt. Both these signs can be detected using GPS.

Working with Radar

A system known as Interferometric Synthetic Aperture Radar (InSAR) has also been developed by engineers to help us look out for earthquakes and volcanoes. It compares radar images of the same place but taken at different times. The images can show if the ground has moved upward slightly. That can indicate movement beneath the surface, which could lead to an earthquake. It can also show changes in the shape of a volcano, which may indicate that an eruption could happen.

Tracking Heat

Thermal imaging cameras are often used to monitor volcanoes. They use heat to find an object. The camera shows the hottest or coldest parts of that object. When monitoring volcanoes, the cameras are used to record the heat level and where the heat is. That is useful because temperatures around a volcano rise if there is more magma activity beneath the surface.

Satellite views of volcanoes can also provide important information when they do erupt. This image shows a volcano erupting on the island of La Palma, off the coast of Africa.

Mapping Danger

Scientists use the information they gather about volcanoes from satellites, radar, and thermal imaging to build up a picture of areas that are at particular risk of volcanic eruptions. They then feed that data into computers to create hazard maps. These are detailed maps of volcanic areas that show the risk of lava flow, ash fall, and pyroclastic flows. They also help show where volcanic mudflows, called lahars, might occur. All that information can be used to figure out what settlements may be at risk if an eruption does take place.

ENGINEERING SOLUTIONS

There is often little anyone can do to protect structures from a powerful volcanic eruption, which can destroy anything in its path. However, engineers try to design buildings that are as resilient as they can be. That means using materials such as reinforced concrete that can handle a buildup of hot and heavy ash. The material is also better able to deal with the heat and pressure of an explosion. Buildings created with such materials are becoming more commonplace in volcanic areas.

Another ingenious engineering invention for monitoring volcanoes and their possible threats are robotic spiders. These devices travel down the sides of volcanoes to survey the level of activity inside them.

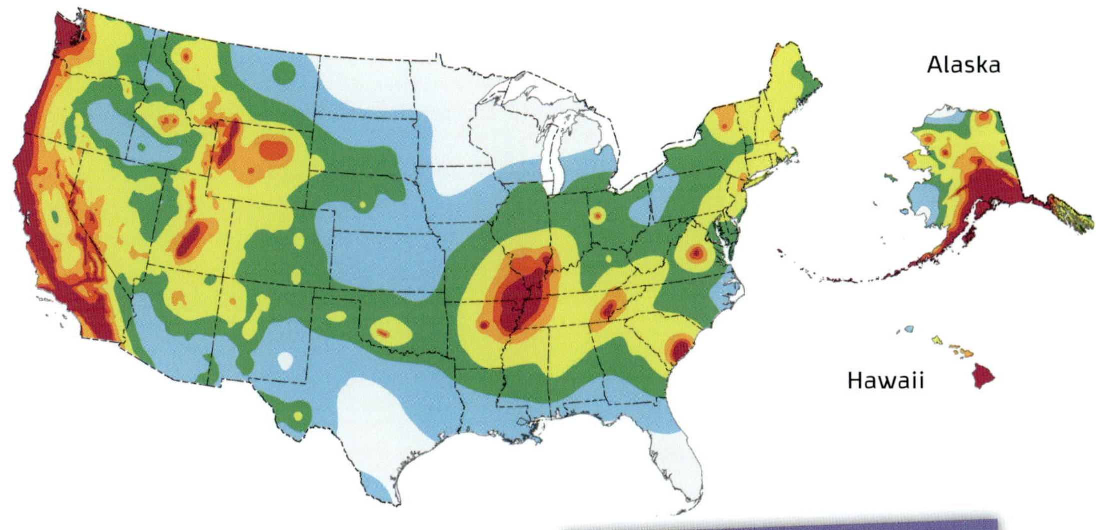

This map of the United States shows where earthquake activity is most likely to take place. The areas in red show places most likely to experience an earthquake, while areas in blue and white are least likely to experience earthquakes.

Monitoring Rivers

Engineers often put in place sensors that measure the flow of sediment in rivers near volcanoes. If a heavy buildup of sediment is detected, it can show that lahars are a risk. Debris basins are useful in places that are at risk of lahars. These are areas that can capture volcanic mudflows, and then redirect them away from nearby settlements. That helps protect buildings and communities.

Making Models

Engineering has also evolved to help us model the likelihood of earthquakes taking place. Seismic hazard models are computer programs that are fed with important information about earthquakes. That includes the history of earthquakes in a region and the faults that may be present. That information is used to build up a picture of how likely it is that an earthquake will occur.

Protecting People

Also fed into a seismic hazard model are the conditions of nearby structures and infrastructure. That includes what homes and other buildings are made of and how they were built. It also includes similar information about important structures such as roads, bridges, and tunnels. That data can be used within the modeling system to predict what would likely happen to those structures if an earthquake took place. The system also predicts how devastating the impact of an earthquake on a region would be, based on its strength. The models created by the system help people figure out what adaptations need to be made to structures to better protect people living in an area in the event of an earthquake.

Building to Save Lives

Earthquakes are very unpredictable. Because of this, most engineering innovations center mainly around making buildings as strong and safe as they can be. Today, engineers also plan areas in earthquake-prone zones to be better able to withstand these powerful forces of nature.

Sadly, many lives are often lost during earthquakes because of poor building practices and the use of unsuitable materials. The structures that people rely on, such as homes, offices, and transportation systems, simply cannot stand up to the force of an earthquake, and crumble. People are caught up and trapped beneath huge amounts of rubble, and many often do not survive. Fires that break out due to damaged gas and electrical supplies are also a hazard to survivors of the quake.

Designed to Defend

Modern building techniques include designing infrastructure such as bridges and roads that are able to withstand an earthquake. Important utility supplies such as gas, electricity, and water systems are all designed to be better at coping with seismic activity. Buildings themselves are designed to stand up to earthquakes and are made from reinforced materials that can survive a quake. That includes using base isolation.

The Quake Breaker room at Te Papa Museum, in New Zealand, displays the base isolator system.

By positioning a pad between the foundation and ground of a building, the shock from an earthquake is absorbed.

HOW IT WORKS:

BASE ISOLATION

Base isolation is a smart way to protect buildings from earthquakes—especially low- to medium-height buildings. It works by placing a flexible pad between the building and the ground. That pad lets the building move gently when the earth shakes, instead of jolting with it.

In physics, there's a rule called inertia. It means that an object will stay still or keep moving the same way unless something forces it to change. During an earthquake, the ground moves suddenly—but if the building is separated from the ground, it doesn't get shaken as hard.

Some isolation systems use lead-rubber bearings. These are made of layers of rubber and steel, with a lead core in the middle. They're very stiff vertically (to hold up the building) but flexible side-to-side. That's important because earthquakes usually shake the ground horizontally.

By letting the building move just enough, base isolation can reduce shaking by up to 75 percent. That helps keep the structure safe—without letting it wobble too much.

Seismic dampers act like shock absorbers for buildings.

Seismic Dampers

Another technology that helps absorb the force of jolts and shakes from earthquakes is the seismic damper. Dampers are like the shock absorbers found in a car or on a mountain bike. In these vehicles, shock absorbers capture some of the energy from jolts so that the driver or rider does not absorb the brunt of the jolt. Seismic dampers work the same way when used in buildings and other structures. When an earthquake hits, some of the seismic energy that travels through the building is absorbed by the dampers. That keeps the structure more stable and means that the building is less likely to collapse.

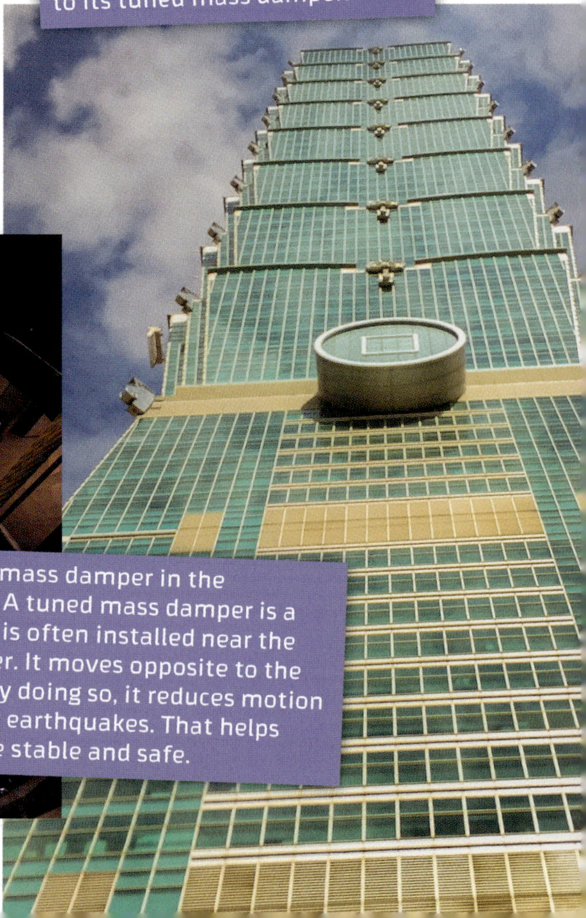

The Taipei 101 Tower is tall but structurally very sound, thanks to its tuned mass damper.

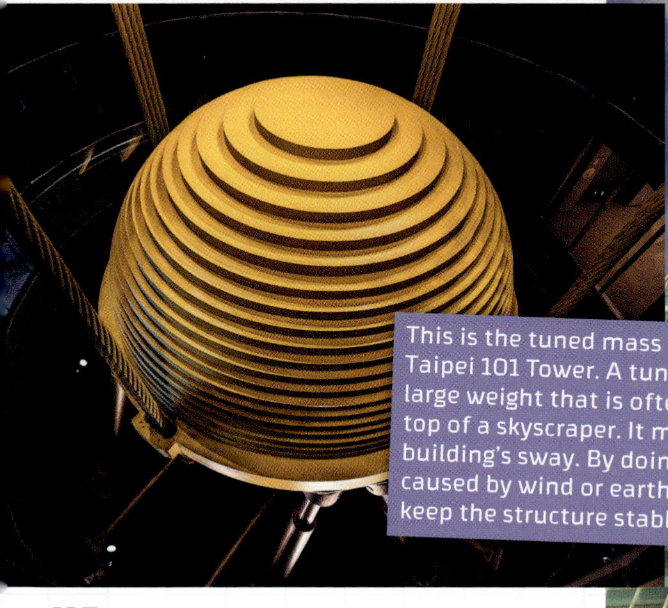

This is the tuned mass damper in the Taipei 101 Tower. A tuned mass damper is a large weight that is often installed near the top of a skyscraper. It moves opposite to the building's sway. By doing so, it reduces motion caused by wind or earthquakes. That helps keep the structure stable and safe.

HOW IT WORKS:
A SHEAR WALL

A shear wall is a strong, vertical wall built inside a building to help it stand firm when the ground shakes or the wind pushes hard from the side. It's designed to resist sideways forces—like those from earthquakes or storms—that could make a building lean, twist, or collapse.

When an earthquake or strong wind hits a building, it pushes sideways against the walls. Regular walls might bend or break under that pressure. But a shear wall is built to stay stiff and strong, so it can:

- Absorb the force of the shaking or wind
- Spread that force downward into the building's foundation
- Keep the building from swaying too much or falling over

Think of it like a brace that holds the building steady—like the spine in your body helps you stand upright. Another way to understand it is as follows: Imagine a tall stack of books. If you push it from the side, it might topple. But if you tape a stiff board to one side, the stack becomes harder to knock over. That board acts like a shear wall—adding strength and stability.

The rods in a shear wall act like the spine in a body: They keep the structure upright even if it is pushed or shaken.

Controlled Rocking Systems

Engineers have discovered that letting a building move slightly during an earthquake can help prevent it from collapsing. That's why they've designed controlled rocking systems. These are special steel frames that are built to rock back and forth on their foundations. The frames are connected in a way that allows the building to tilt slightly when the ground shakes, then return to its original position. Think of it like a punching bag with a weighted bottom—it moves when hit, but springs back upright.

To make controlled rocking systems work, engineers leave a small gap at the base of the building. That gap gives the structure room to rock safely. Inside the system, strong cables and special dampers help absorb the shaking and pull the building back into place. Controlled rocking systems help buildings stay strong and recover quickly after an earthquake—without crumbling under pressure.

CHAPTER 5

TORNADOES AND HURRICANES

Predicting tornadoes and hurricanes relies on sophisticated engineering tools. Unlike hurricanes, which can be tracked as they form, tornadoes develop very quickly. And they often do so with very little warning. However, there are certain devices that help people figure out when and where they are likely to take place.

The tornado that struck Wray, Colorado, in 2016 was rated EF2.

Storm Prediction

Doppler radar can detect the rotation of large amounts of air, which can be a sign of a forming tornado. Meteorologists know that large rotating thunderstorms are supercells that can spawn tornadoes. By measuring the movement of rotating air, it is possible to pinpoint these superstorms. Meteorologists also use radar to identify a special echo within a storm. A hook-shaped radar echo is linked to storms that often produce tornadoes. Engineers have developed special algorithms that identify these echo patterns, which help meteorologists predict tornadoes.

Sending Out Pulses

Another form of radar that helps identify tornadoes is dual-polarization radar. This sends out horizontal and vertical pulses. They help distinguish between types of particles in the air. When debris is lifted into a tornado, the radar can detect it. The data helps scientists confirm that a tornado is on the way and on the ground, even if it cannot immediately be seen. The radar also helps measure the amount of rain, hail, and snow in the storm. That helps scientists figure out how powerful the storm is, which provides more information about the size and possible behavior of a tornado.

Checking from Above

Satellites in space are also powerful tools in tracking and monitoring tornadoes. They allow scientists to watch for rapidly growing thunderstorms and particular types of clouds, which can all be signs that tornadoes are on the way. Infrared imaging on satellites helps detect changes in storm clouds too. Weather balloons contain sensors that measure temperature, humidity, and pressure at different heights. That information helps meteorologists figure out how stable air is and how much moisture it contains. Both factors influence storms and the development of tornadoes.

Satellites are also used to monitor hurricanes. They provide images that enable scientists to track the size, movement, and intensity of tropical storms and hurricanes. Sensors on satellites measure cloud temperature, rainfall, and the temperature of the sea surface. All of which are important for predicting hurricanes

ENGINEERING SOLUTIONS

Monitoring tornadoes from the ground is also important, but difficult. Scientists use ground-based sensors to measure wind speed and direction. These measurements help provide scientists with information about wind shear, which is an important part of tornado formation. However, unless the sensors are up close to a tornado, the information they can provide is limited. That's where portable radars come in. These transportable devices are used on vehicles by people who follow and track tornadoes. They are called storm chasers. As the storm chasers travel toward tornadoes, the radars gather real-time data about wind speed, pressure, humidity, and the temperature inside storms. That provides scientists with valuable information about tornadoes and how they form.

Supercell storms, like this one over the Colorado plains, look ominous.

Hunting Hurricanes

Scientists are using devices that operate a little like drones to study hurricanes. They are called dropsondes. They travel into the storms and collect data. Planes called hurricane hunters carry the dropsondes and drop them inside the storm. The devices are equipped with sensors that collect data about the storm. That data includes wind speed, air pressure, temperature, and humidity. The dropsondes can also measure low-altitude turbulence in the middle of the storm. Scientists and engineers hope to use this data to create models that can better predict the intensity of these storms when they form.

The dropsondes have GPS technology on board, so they can transmit their position every half second as they drop through the storm toward the ocean. On one flight alone, 20 dropsondes may fly into a storm at various spots. By doing so, information about the storm from its eye to its outer rim can be gathered and sent to scientists on the ground.

Working on the Water

The hurricane hunters can also drop special floats onto the surface of the ocean. The floats measure the water temperature, surface wind, and wave height of the ocean under the storm. And there are also drones that work specifically on water. They are called saildrones. Rather than flying into the storm, they sail into it. There, they collect data on wind speed, air temperature, and humidity. They also measure atmospheric pressure, currents, and wave heights.

Hurricane hunters provide vital information about hurricanes. They help scientists better understand and predict these powerful and destructive storms.

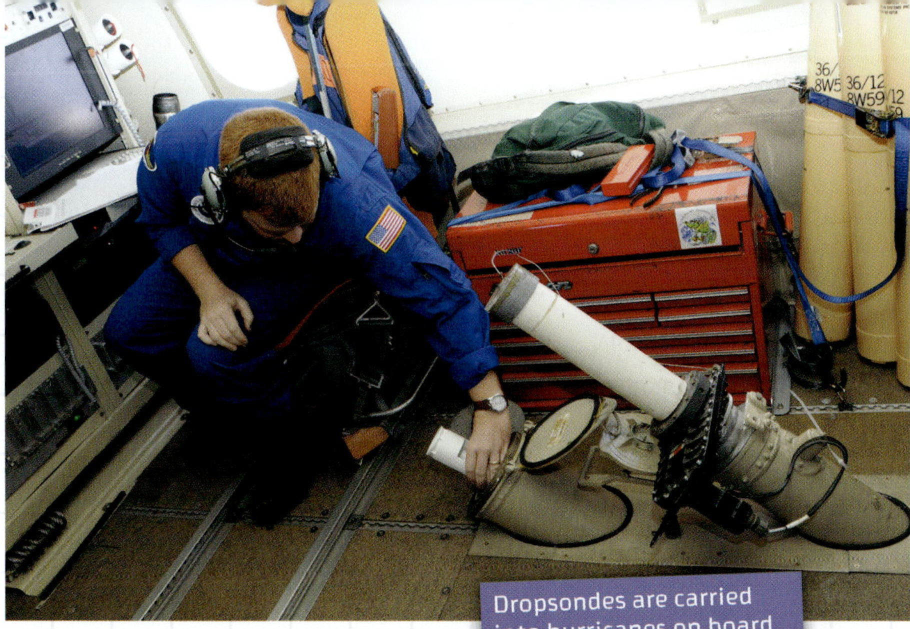

Dropsondes are carried into hurricanes on board aircraft like this one, then dropped into the storm to study it and send data.

Storms and Supercomputers

Meteorologists use powerful computers to analyze all the billions of pieces of data they collect about weather. They use the data from dropsondes, saildrones, satellites, and radar systems and feed it into the supercomputers. That information is then used to create forecast models that enable scientists to predict what storms will do. The models are a little like pretend storms, and they allow scientists to predict the path of a hurricane. That enables meteorologists to warn people that a hurricane is heading in their direction, so they can evacuate before it hits land.

Governments and emergency services rely on prediction data to prepare for approaching storms. Although no prediction is 100 percent accurate, the information does help emergency services mobilize resources where needed. It also helps officials encourage people to follow a safety plan that could save their lives.

ENGINEERING SOLUTIONS

Tornadoes can be unpredictable, and their movements can quickly change. Trying to figure out what they are likely to do can be very difficult, but computer modeling is helping. Computer models are used to simulate weather conditions. That helps with predicting and understanding tornadoes. The High-Resolution Rapid Refresh (HRRR) model is one of the most effective. It can create multiple model simulations, each with a slight variation. That helps meteorologists figure out how weather conditions may affect tornado patterns.

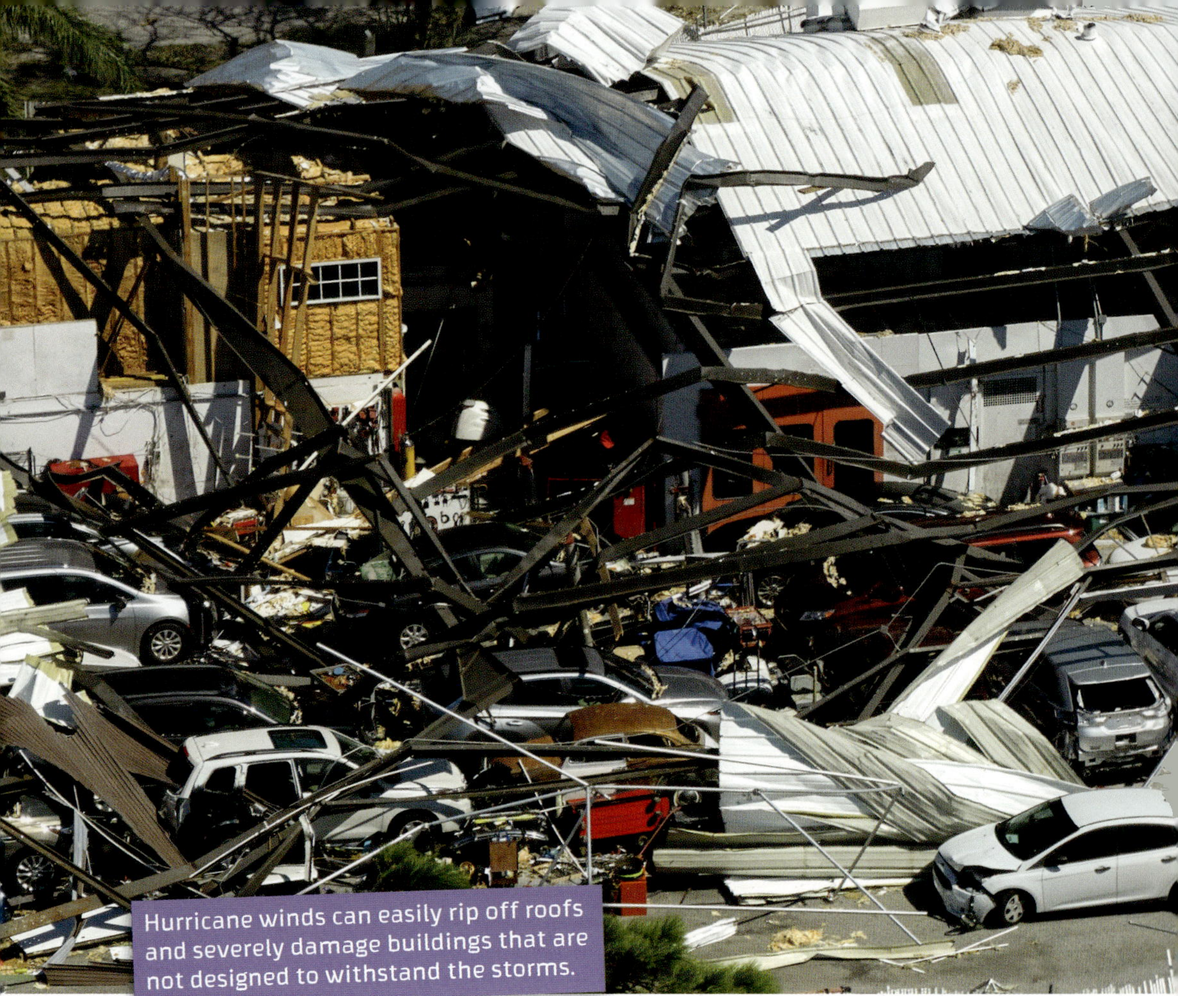

Hurricane winds can easily rip off roofs and severely damage buildings that are not designed to withstand the storms.

Billion-Dollar Storms

Hurricanes and tornadoes have been responsible for billions of dollars of damage in recent years. They have also cost thousands of lives. Building structures that can withstand these awesome forces of nature is a challenge but engineering is underway to try to make the structures that people rely on sounder and safer.

Holding Back the Water

When a hurricane hits, holding back the water that comes from storm surges and heavy rainfall is essential. Retractable flood barriers are proving especially useful in urban areas that are often affected by hurricanes, such as New Orleans. The barriers can be raised temporarily to protect against storm surges, then lowered again when not needed. Many coastal cities now have improved seawalls, breakwater walls, and levees to provide a barrier between the sea and the city. Engineers now employ more and more green ideas in their protection systems too. These involve preserving natural barriers such as mangrove forests and dunes, which naturally absorb storm surges and help prevent flooding.

Building Better

In areas that experience a lot of storms, power lines are often buried deep underground to protect them from driving winds. That reduces the chance of power outages during a hurricane. Roads and bridges are also designed and built to be able to withstand the storms, with tougher, reinforced materials that can hold out against heavy rain and high winds.

Buildings in areas that are frequently visited by tornadoes are now also designed with reinforced walls and foundations. They are made from materials that are tough, such as concrete and steel. Windows and doors are reinforced too, and laminated glass and storm shutters are often used. Homes in hurricane-prone states such as Florida are now built to survive the storms. They are equipped with hurricane shutters, reinforced doors, and impact-resistant windows. Roof straps or hurricane clips that connect the roof to the basement or concrete slab are also required. The clips are also used on buildings that lie in tornado-risk areas, such as the Midwest.

HOW IT WORKS:
A HURRICANE CLIP

Hurricane clips are an important protection against windstorms like hurricanes or tornadoes. Roofs are prone to flying off buildings in severe wind events because of the uplift the wind creates under the edges of the roof. The wind rushing below the edges of the roof can create enough pressure to lift it off if it is not properly secured. This is where hurricane clips can help.

Hurricane clips are far tougher and more effective in keeping roofs attached than traditional nails.

Hurricane clips are metal plates that bolt the roof truss to the beams of the house. The roof truss is made up of triangular beams that build the peak of the house, underneath the shingles or tiles. Normally, the truss is bolted onto the house beams with large nails. However, the nails are no match for hurricane- or tornado-force winds. The plates used for hurricane clips bolt into both the truss and the house beams and are made of steel. The clips are designed to withstand winds of over 100 miles per hour (160 kph).

CHAPTER 6

ENGINEERING AFTER DISASTER

Engineering is as important after a natural disaster has taken place as it is before it. Disasters usually wreak havoc among communities. Homes and workplaces are destroyed. So too are schools, hospitals, and other important public buildings. People's access to electricity and gas to cook with, provide light in the dark, and provide warmth against cold disappears. Clean drinking water is often also removed. All these harmful consequences can put people in very vulnerable positions. They are at risk of disease due to poor sanitary conditions and may lack basic shelter and food. Today, the work of engineers is vitally important to bring rescue and recovery efforts to people affected by natural disasters.

A Helping Hand

Helping survivors after a natural disaster is a complex and skilled operation. It can mean rescuing people from damaged buildings, which often requires specialized equipment. It includes providing temporary water supply systems with smart purification technology, so people have clean water. One of the main causes of death from natural disasters is a lack of clean drinking water. Dirty water carries bugs that cause diseases such as cholera, and many people die because of disease after a disaster rather than the disaster itself. Installing temporary sewage systems is also very important. Innovative engineering means that easy-to-assemble public toilets with suitable sanitary systems can be put in place quickly after a disaster. That too reduces the risk of disease.

Temporary shelters that can be quickly erected after a disaster are an important engineering solution.

Drones can take photographs of earthquake damage over a wide area. That provides rescue and rebuild operators with vital information.

ENGINEERING SOLUTIONS

Quickly assessing the scale of damage after a natural disaster is vital to stop further destruction and help rescue efforts. That can be very difficult to do on land. Transportation systems are often affected, making travel difficult. Infrastructure may also be damaged and unstable. The best way to carry out surveillance is from the air. Drones equipped with cameras and sensors are used to make surveys of affected areas from the sky. That bird's eye view and the images captured help people quickly figure out the level of damage to roads, bridges, buildings, and other important structures. Satellite imagery is also used to determine the extent of damage over a large area.

Rebuilding and Restoring

After immediate needs are met, engineering makes it possible to restore communities and rebuild settlements. And that needs to be done in a way that makes them resilient to future disasters. Engineering knowledge now means that people understand what materials perform better under stress. Those components include high-performance concrete, fiber-reinforced materials, and seismic-resistant technology. All those state-of-the art engineering systems and materials can be used to rebuild areas devastated by natural disasters.

Using prefabricated and advanced modular building techniques also means that temporary or permanent housing can be put up. That also applies to schools and other important buildings such as hospitals. Using these powerful engineering tools and ideas means that people affected by devastating natural disasters have a chance of recovering from them much more quickly.

Tackling the Environment

Predicting natural disasters and coming up with innovative solutions for managing them are very important. They help limit the damage and loss of life that all too often result from powerful natural events. However, exciting developments are taking place in another area, too: addressing the environmental factors behind these natural events. While we will never be able to stop storms like hurricanes and tornadoes, scientists and engineers are looking for solutions to try to minimize these weather events. And they are coming up with many smart ways to better manage other natural disasters such as wildfires, tsunamis, earthquakes, and volcanoes.

Monitoring the effect of global warming and climate change on our planet, and making efforts to control it, will be key in helping lessen further natural disasters such as tornadoes and hurricanes.

Stopping the Storms

Scientists have considered the idea of creating a "sunglass effect" to cool the planet. This strategy involves pumping sulfate gases into the upper atmosphere. These dense gases can absorb some wavelengths of light, which would reduce the energy that reaches and warms the oceans. Think of it like sunglasses: They block the harmful rays from reaching a person's eyes, and would block the harmful rays from warming the oceans.

Scientists believe this method would be effective because when volcanoes have erupted and given off sulfur dioxide, the following storm season typically has less powerful storms. Scientists claim they could cut the number of massive hurricanes in half over the coming years by using a sunglass effect. However, there are environmental concerns about this method because it could change climate in ways that could be harmful to both ecosystems and agriculture.

Using a Cloak

Another innovative approach to earthquake safety is the development of seismic cloaking. A seismic cloak is placed around a structure to absorb and redirect the surface seismic waves that come from an earthquake and that are most likely to cause damage. The cloaking materials redirect the energy from the earthquake away from buildings and to the surrounding area. Scientists are still experimenting with what materials can best be used for cloaking.

HOW IT WORKS: COOLING THE OCEANS

We know that hurricanes are fueled by the warm waters found in tropical and subtropical ocean areas. As these waters get even warmer, hurricanes will become more frequent and intense. Scientists are wondering if there is a way to cool the oceans. One company, OceanTherm, is working on an idea to use "bubble curtains" to cool the surface temperature of the water.

The surface temperature of the tropical and subtropical ocean waters is warm. However, as you go deeper into the water, the temperature drops. OceanTherm wants to use a series of underwater pipes to force pressurized air down into the deeper part of the ocean. This would create bubbles that would force the colder water from the depths of the ocean up to the surface. That would cool the overall surface temperature of the water. Without the "food" of the warm surface water, the hurricane will not be able to develop into such a devastating storm.

THE FUTURE IS EVOLVING

Engineers are creative problem-solvers. Through inventive solutions, they have lessened the risks associated with natural disasters. Natural disasters are something that people will continue to have to live with, especially as global climate change continues to alter our planet. But engineers will continue to find ways to limit the risk these natural disasters present to people and property. Perhaps they will even find ways that we can use these occurrences to our benefit. Imagine if we could use some of the powerful energy of nature to help solve one of our other pressing problems: our energy crisis.

Could we use wind turbines to capture the energy of storms?

Wind Turbines to Slow the Storm

Engineer Mark Jacobson of Stanford University has come up with the idea of installing huge wind farms in the oceans where hurricanes form. These farms would have tens of thousands of wind turbines offshore. As a hurricane moves into the area, the turbines would slow the winds.

Jacobson has created simulations that explain how the wind turbines might work. One of them showed what would have happened if 79,000 turbines had been installed in the Gulf of Mexico directly in the path of Hurricane Katrina, which hit land in 2005. The turbines would have reduced the windspeed of the hurricane's winds by 80 to 100 miles per hour (128 to 160 kph). They would have decreased the water volume produced by the storm by 79 percent. And not only would the turbines have slowed the wind, but they would also have captured its energy too. That energy could be used to create electricity that we can use to power our buildings, machines, and vehicles.

HOW IT WORKS:

WIND FARMS SLOWING DOWN WINDS

You might wonder how wind farms could possibly lower the windspeed in a weather event such as a hurricane. You are probably also wondering how they create electricity. The answer can be found in the laws of physics. The wind has kinetic energy. As it moves past a wind turbine, some of that kinetic energy is dedicated to moving the blades of the turbine. That absorbs the energy of the wind and generates electricity. The kinetic energy from the wind is not destroyed —it is instead transformed into useful electrical energy.

EVOLVE AS AN ENGINEER

Intelligent engineering solutions require smart, creative brains. Great engineering minds of the past taught us to build levees and dams to manage water. Engineering has helped us build hurricane- and tornado-safe structures that can withstand high winds. It has allowed us to make buildings that can flex as Earth shakes. The exciting field of engineering can also be incredibly rewarding, particularly when you are a part of solutions that will benefit the planet. If you would like to build an engineering career, explore the following pages to discover how you could work in this field. In doing so, you could help find more ways to deal with natural disasters.

EVOLVING CAREERS IN ENGINEERING

For would-be engineers, there are many exciting job opportunities within the realm of natural disasters. Here are just some of the evolving engineering roles you could explore if you're interested in using science to lower the risks of natural disasters.

Civil Engineer

Civil engineers work on the design, construction, and maintenance of buildings and other infrastructure projects, such as roads, bridges, airports, and water supply systems. They apply engineering principles to ensure that projects are safe, structurally sound, sustainable, and environmentally friendly. Response to natural disasters often focuses on making sure that buildings and infrastructure will remain safe in the event of a disaster, so engineers are vital in this field.

Environmental Engineer

Natural disasters are impacted by climate change and the environment. If we can get climate change under control, we will limit, to some extent, the scope of future natural disasters. Environmental engineers are a valuable part of the team for that reason. In designing environmentally conscious solutions, they help keep us safer. And they can design solutions for disasters that may ultimately bring some benefit from the destruction.

If you are interested in natural disasters, civil engineering could be a great field for you.

Collecting and analyzing soil samples is part of the job of a geotechnical engineer.

Mechanical Engineer

Mechanical engineers work in different areas. That is because their expertise means they can design, develop, build, and maintain many different mechanical sensor devices. Sensors are a big factor in storm detection and early warning systems. If that is an area that interests you, you might want to consider mechanical engineering as a career.

Geotechnical Engineer

Geotechnical engineers study the geological conditions of Earth, including the rocks and soil. They are very important in the world of natural disasters because structures are built from the ground up. If the ground below a structure such as a building, bridge, or water catchment basin is not structurally sound, it could result in major damage if a natural disaster took place. For example, in earthquake-prone areas, geotechnical engineers look at the features of Earth's crust when planning buildings. They then determine whether the building site is a safe place to build on.

Software Engineer

Most of the prediction tools and early warning systems for natural disasters use computers and other electronics. Modeling software and simulations are also increasingly used to try to predict outcomes from natural disasters. If this is an area that interests you, you might want to consider software engineering.

How to Get into Engineering

If you think some or all of the roles outlined on the previous pages could be for you, the next steps in building a career in engineering start at school. Focus on STEM subjects because you will need qualifications in this area. STEM includes science, technology, engineering, and math. Engineers use math to problem solve and figure out designs, so it is an important skill to work on. Science is important too, because you'll need to understand physical science concepts such as forces, energy, and materials.

STEM Clubs and Camps

Consider joining a STEM club. This is a great place to work on your engineering skills. Many schools have clubs that focus on robotics, coding, and engineering challenges. Taking part will give you important hands-on experience that will help set you up for a career in engineering. You could also try a STEM camp. Many summer camps are STEM-focused today, to help young people develop these important skills. You can also explore the many STEM-focused online camps and classes available if you don't find an in-person one near you.

Consider Coding and Kits

Many areas of engineering require coding skills, so working on understanding the basics of coding is a great way to get into engineering. Try platforms such as Scratch, Python, or Blockly. Programming is very important in engineering fields such as robotics and electrical engineering. You can also work on simple projects such as games, apps, and easy robots to put what you have learned into practice. Having fun with kits can also help build your engineering skills. Try working with LEGO™, Arduino, and similar kits to build robots, electronic devices, and gadgets. Any practical work like this will fire up your engineering brain and show you how exciting this area can be.

STEM and robotics clubs and camps are great places to get some hands-on engineering experience.

Talk to Other Engineers

Tell your teachers that you are interested in engineering, and they may be able to put you in touch with engineers who could talk to you about career options. You may even be able to visit engineers at work and see what a day in the life in this career is like. School counselors are also great people to talk to about career options, and they may be able to find engineering mentors for you to talk to. They will also be able to advise on courses to take once you finish school that will help you land a career in engineering.

Find Out More

When thinking about the next steps after school, spend time researching engineering programs at colleges and universities. The more you can find out now, the better placed you will be when the time comes to apply for a course.

There are different types of engineering, like mechanical, electrical, civil, aerospace, and environmental engineering. Each one leads to different kinds of jobs, so exploring your options early can help you decide what interests you most. Many colleges offer open days, online tours, and information sessions so you can see what their programs are like and ask questions.

GLOSSARY

Age of Enlightenment a period of time in the seventeenth and eighteenth centuries in which huge advances were made in science

algorithms sets of rules to be followed when making calculations or problem-solving

ancient Egyptians a civilization that existed between 3100 and 30 BCE

ancient Greeks an advanced ancient civilization that lived in Greece around 2,500 years ago. The ancient Greeks developed a civilization that was rich in art, politics, engineering, and other forms of science

artificial intelligence (AI) software that performs tasks that normally require human intelligence

atmosphere the protective layers of gas that surround Earth

Aztecs people belonging to a civilization that lived in Central Mexico between 1300 and 1521 CE

barometer a tool used to measure atmospheric pressure

braced made stronger and firmer

buoy a float that is anchored by a weight and placed on a body of water

channels lengths of water that join larger areas of water

cholera a disease caused by bacteria that live in water

civic planning the design and planning of areas used by people, such as towns and cities

civilizations societies that have a particular culture and way of life

climate change long-term shifts in temperature and weather patterns

condenses causes a gas to change into a liquid

crust the outermost layer of the planet. Earth is made up of a series of layers. The crust is the outer layer. The mantle is the layer that sits beneath it, and beneath the mantle is the outer core. The inner core is the innermost layer

dams strong barriers created to hold back water

data information

debris remains of something

dense relates to how compact something is

dikes long walls built to prevent flooding

downdraft a downward current of air

drainage a means of removing extra water or liquid waste

dugouts trenches dug into the ground and often covered with roofs for shelter

durability the ability to last a long time

elasticity describes how easily something stretches and then returns to its former shape

emissions substances released into the air

environmental relating to the natural world and the impact of human activity on it

environmentally conscious concerned with the environment and the impact of human activity on it

equator an imaginary line around the center of Earth

estimate to make a guess based on fact
evacuate to move people away from areas of danger
evidence facts or information that can support whether something is true
evolved developed gradually from a simple to a more complex form
fertile capable of producing crops or vegetation
firebreaks obstacles that can stop a fire spreading
flammable easily catches fire
flexible able to easily bend
foundation the lowest load-bearing part of a building. Usually the base on which a buildings lies
geostationary describes an object above Earth that moves with the planet's rotation, so that it appears to be fixed at a certain point in the sky
global warming the overall increase in the temperature of Earth's atmosphere, which scientists believe is increasing due to greenhouse gas emissions
humidity the amount of water vapor in the atmosphere
Incas people belonging to a civilization that developed into a great empire in South America between 1438 and 1533 CE
Indus Valley Civilization a people who lived in northwestern parts of South Asia between 3300 and 1300 BCE
infrared relating to rays like light but which cannot be seen
ingenious very smart and not thought of before
inhabitants people who live somewhere
innovations new methods, ideas, or products
interlocking joining together by overlapping
irrigation the supply of water to land or crops
kinetic related to motion
lava molten rock when it reaches Earth's surface
levees structures built around a river to stop it overflowing
mangrove forests areas of trees that have long roots that reach into salt water and that can withstand saltwater conditions
Maya a powerful civilization that lived in Central America between 300 and 900 CE
Medieval related to a period of time that lasted from around 500 to 1500 CE
Mesopotamians an ancient civilization that existed in what is now Iraq between 600 and 400 BCE
Midwest the region of northern states in the United States that extends from the Rocky Mountains east to Ohio
minerals nonliving substances that have a particular chemical makeup
Minoan a civilization that existed on the island of Crete in what is now Greece from about 3000 to 1100 BCE
modular items that can be easily rearranged to suit different needs
momentum gathering speed of movement
mortar a substance used to join pieces of stone or bricks to form a structure. Mortar is applied when it is wet and as it dries, it fixes surrounding materials into position
nutritious contains a lot of nutrients, which are substances needed for good health
orbit to move around another body, such as a planet
particles small pieces

porous having small spaces or holes through which air or liquid can pass

power outages breaks in the supply of power such as electricity, often caused by storms

prediction a forecast of what is likely to happen

prefabricated made beforehand in another area and then transported to be put together where needed

purification making pure and clean

pyroclastic flows fast-moving and thick flows of hot ash, lava, and gas from a volcanic eruption

radar a system for detecting the presence, direction, distance, and speed of objects. Radar works by sending out pulses of radio waves that reflect off the surface of objects

reclaim to take back

reinforced made stronger and more resilient

Renaissance a period of history in Europe that lasted from the fifteenth century to the sixteenth century. During that period, great advances in science and art were made

reservoirs large, enclosed bodies of water that are kept in reserve for use during times when water is not easily available

resilient able to withstand pressure

retention ponds pools of water designed to take in additional water created during storms and floods

retractable can be pulled back

rigid fixed and unable to easily bend

sanitary relates to cleanliness

sediment small pieces of stone or earth

sensors devices that detect or measure things in the environment

settlements places where groups of people live

stormwater runoff rain or melted snow that runs across the land during a storm

stormwater drainage a system that drains stormwater away from areas where it could cause damage

subtropical near the tropics

surveillance watching and monitoring

sustainable able to be maintained at a certain rate or level

taper becomes slimmer at one end

tempered glass glass that is made tougher and able to withstand pressure and heat

terrain land with particular geographic features, such as rivers and mountains

thermometer a tool used to measure temperature

trenches long, narrow ditches

tropical relating to the tropics, which are parts of Earth found near the equator

turbulence violent, unsteady movements of air

updraft an upward current of air

urban related to towns and cities

ventilation the provision of clean, fresh air to a building

water vapor water that has turned into a gas

weather forecasting predicting the weather

wind farms areas in which many wind turbines are set up to capture the wind's energy

wind pressure the pressure on a structure exerted by wind

wind shear the difference in wind speed and direction over a short distance

FIND OUT MORE

Books

Estes, Fred. *Teen Innovators: Nine Young People Engineering a Better World with Creative Inventions*. Zest Books, 2022.

Salt, Rachel. *Is it Weather or Is It Climate Change? Answers to Your Questions About Extreme Weather*. Firefly Books, 2024.

Taylor, Diane. *The Science of Natural Disasters: When Nature and Humans Collide*. Nomad Press, 2020.

Websites

Read about the biggest natural disasters in history at:
www.livescience.com/biggest-natural-disasters-throughout-history

This online game produced by the United Nations Office for Disaster Risk Reduction allows teens and adults to explore how to build safer cities and villages in the face of disasters:
www.stopdisastersgame.org

Solve problems through science and engineering on this interactive site:
https://xplorlabs.org

Publisher's note to educators and parents:
All the websites featured above have been carefully reviewed to ensure that they are suitable for students. However, many websites change often, and we cannot guarantee that a site's future contents will continue to meet our high standards of educational value. Please be advised that students should be closely monitored whenever they access the Internet.

INDEX

ABOUT THE AUTHORS

Sarah Eason and Cathleen Small have written a wide variety of books for teens, including many STEM titles.